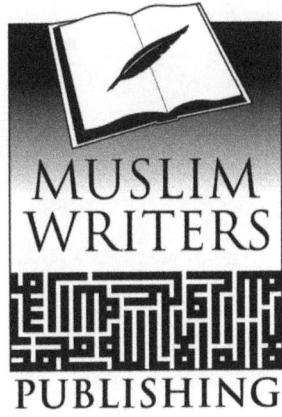

Many Poetic Voices, One Faith
© 2009 Islamic Writers Alliance

Muslim Writers Publishing
PO Box 27362
Tempe, Arizona 85285

www.MuslimWritersPublishing.com

ISBN: 978-0-9819770-0-3

Islamic Writers Alliance
PO Box 299
Sunbury, Pennsylvania 17801

www.islamicwritersalliance.net

Cover Art by Nazaahah Amin
Interior Illustrations by Shirley Gavin Anjum
Book Design by Leila Joiner
Editing by Leila Joiner

Printed in the United States of America

Many Poetic Voices,
One Faith

Islamic Writers Alliance

We Write What We Believe...
and We Believe in What We Write!

INTRODUCTION BY MAHASIN D. SHAMSID-DEEN,
IWA ASSISTANT DIRECTOR

The Islamic Writers Alliance annual poetry contest has been a phenomenon that lends meaning to the saying of Prophet Muhammad (Prayers and Peace be upon him) that in poetry there is some wisdom.

Practically every type of poetry has been submitted for the annual contests, including acoustics, ballads, cinquain, couplets, epics, elegy, free verse, ghazal, haiku, narrative, ode sonnet, and many more, including youth's favorite, abc and even spoken word.

Poets from every continent, excluding Antarctica, have participated in the contest. Each year an Islamic school from the U.S., UK, or Canada has a class to take the contest on as a project. There are as many men poets as women, and the topics have been an artistic expression of the heartfelt love and agony of the writers. The result has been a poetic triumphant communication of varied spirituality, history, angst, politics, love, and faith, as beautiful and colorful, varied and expressive, and naturally occurring as that of the northern lights or aurora borealis.

The contest first took place in 2005. The theme was open, and the response was reflective of the earlier stages of the IWA development. Still, the winning poem was thought-provoking in its analogy. Judges for the year were themselves poets.

When the second year of the contest came in 2006, the IWA board was faced with wanting to have a positive response to the unfortunate Jylland Postem cartoon controversy that occurred in the fall of 2005. Muslims worldwide were deeply offended, and protests and, unfortunately in some cases, deaths resulted. Therefore, the theme of

"Prophet Muhammad" (SAW) was chosen for the contestants to share their love, thoughts, and reflections. Alhamdulillah, the response was tremendous from all over the world and was actually, to date, the only poetry contest where both Muslim and non-Muslims participated as contestants and were approached as judges.

In 2007 the annual poetry contest was open again and netted poems that spoke on politics, religion, hijab, and injustice. This was the year that a spoken word writing on poverty received an honorable mention, thus expanding the poetry contest genre even further.

In 2008 the IWA board decided to shake things up a bit and held a public voting contest – after all, poetry is meant to be read and appreciated by the masses. A blog was put up at the website, and people could read the poems in each category, and then vote for whichever one they liked. The theme of Iman – Faith was chosen to not only help writers stay on an Islamic topic, but to help readers focus on one thought pattern. The poets themselves missed the evaluation of their work from published authors this year, but this format was particularly exciting to youth contestants.

For the fifth year, the IWA choose to have an open theme contest for the contestants. As in the past, submissions came from all over the globe on every topic, with a surprisingly higher than usual focus on women's issues outside of hijab in the poetry.

Insha'Allah, the Islamic Writers Alliance will continue to have a poetry contest, and each year we pray that the annual poetry contest continues to grow and inspire poets to let the ink flow on the paper, as the thoughts and passion flows within their hearts.

TABLE OF CONTENTS

Islamic Writers Alliance
1st Annual Poetry Contest
Member Award Winning Poem
2005

Olives Under Stones by Corey Habbas
2005 IWA Member Category Winner

Flint escapes this land of
Bani Na'im, the flicker
that her eyes once held
when rubbed dim with ash
isn't me yet.

Who churns the olives now
that caterpillars have ground
the homes to paste and
butterflies don't dance.
I knew of a

Climbing-tree full of fruit
where blossoms pushed
olive meat out over seed
a black cocoon stuffed
with promise

I could be any woman now
encased within a wall, looking
out through thorny barbs and
metal brambles, a butterfly
not meant to escape

The stones that come
for her from Pene Hever, as
the groves convulse, won't
welcome her into the gates of
Saragossa

Allah, maintain the peace
in our hearts, that with the olives
they pilfer, show me the path
within my soul that leads
to righteousness

Show me in your nature,
in her harvest, in the twisting
of charred olive branches, the path
to take forgiveness, that caterpillars,
which burnish women to sand
Fly over me as butterflies might

she casts her eyes to
the Sacred Rock and we will
invite them all into the gates of Saragossa
in the spirit of a
shared Jerusalem.

Corey Habbas, a Muslim revert since 2000 and freelance writer, has had her writing published in various online and print journals, newspapers, and magazines. Her short stories and articles for children have been featured in *Learning Through History Magazine* and *Skipping Stones*. Corey has won several awards for her poetry, including prizes from the Islamic Writers Alliance and Qalaam. In 2006, her poetry won the Andalusia Prize for Literature. Corey grew up in California, where she studied art and also earned her Bachelor of Science degree in Information Systems from the University of Redlands. Corey also authored the Islamic fiction book, *The Runaway Scarf*, in 2008. She now lives in Minnesota with her family. She is a member of the Islamic Writers Alliance.

MANY THANKS TO OUR JUDGES

Dasham Brookins, MuslimPoet.com
Isla Roser-Owen, Qalam
Eman Tai, *Calligraphy of Thought*
Pamela Taylor, IWA Publications Officer

Islamic Writers Alliance
2nd Annual Poetry Contest
Award Winning Poetry
2006

Muhammad by Karen English
2006 IWA Member Category Winner

Muhammad
They kept his name from us,
swaddled it in cotton,
tied it in a box,
buried that box deep in the earth.
Away from our eyes,
so tightly the secret of his name was kept.
But then something nudged us
A germ of distant memory,
a single grain at first
With time's breath fanning it more into life
---slowly---
as a morning dawning.
What was it? What was it?
Know your God is One?
Fall down in adoration
of that One?
We remembered—
those who came before us
on angry seas,
faces pressed to the ship's deck,
over and over.
Why?
We remembered---
our grandmothers
before the sun rose
faces pressed the cabin's dirt floor.

Why?
Still, they kept his name from us.
Muhammad.
Obscured his message,
tried to extinguish his truth

not knowing the seed was already
buried deep in the soil of our souls.
It had traveled with us,
was destined to perfectly grow.
Until, ---one by one,
ten by ten,
hundreds by hundreds,
thousands upon thousands---
we would bear witness to Muhammad's Message
Know that your God is One
and there is no God but He.

Karen English was born in Vallejo, California in 1947. She grew up in Los Angeles, California with her mother, step-father, brother, and sister. She received her BA in Psychology from California State University at Los Angeles, as well as a teaching credential. Until recently, she taught second grade. She is the mother of four grown children and grandmother of one. She currently lives in Los Angeles. She feels blessed to be a writer and has authored 13 books. Karen says that writing makes life so much more interesting because she sees a story in almost everything.

Awards

- Coretta Scott King Honor Award for FRANCIE
- BABRA Award for FRANCIE
- Parent Choice for FRANCIE
- Judy Lopez Award for FRANCIE
- Jane Addams Award for HOT DAY ON ABBOTT AVENUE

MANY THANKS TO OUR JUDGES

Youth Judge: Rukhsana Khan, author, *Muslim Child*

Adult Judge and IWA Member Judge:
Dasham Brookins, MuslimPoet.com

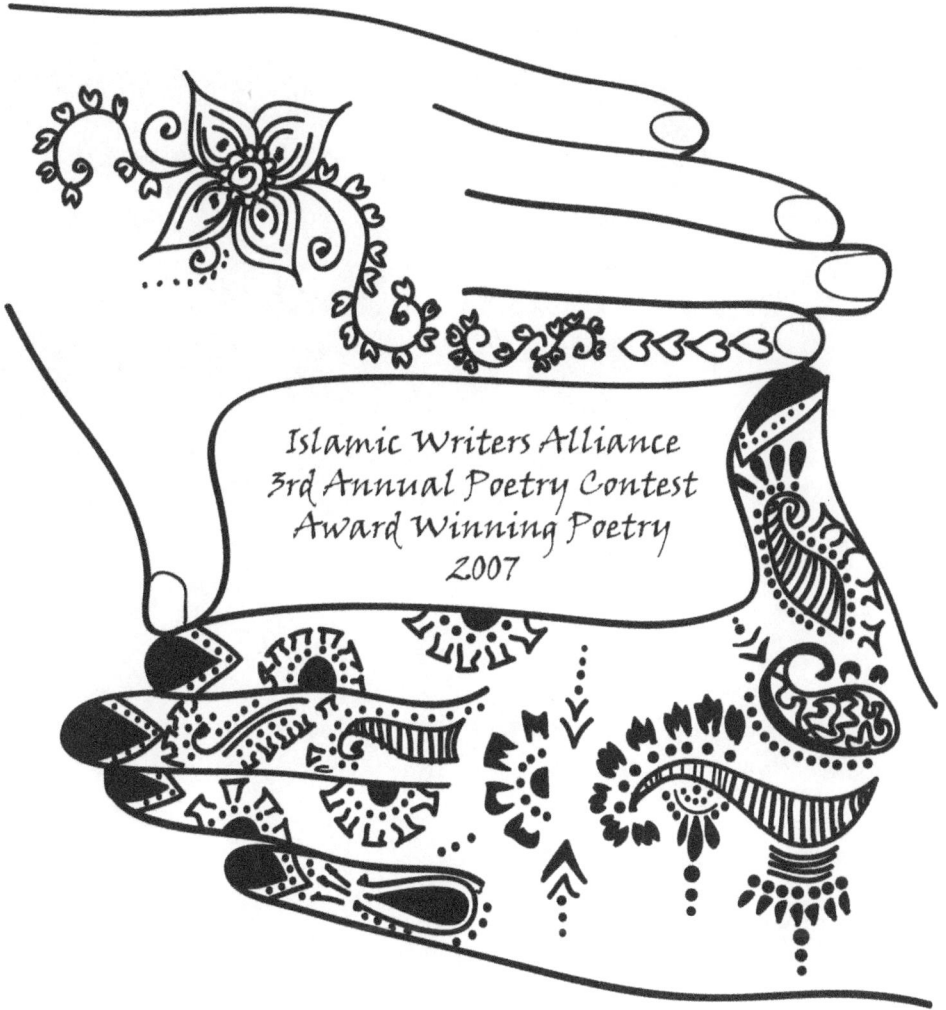

Islamic Writers Alliance
3rd Annual Poetry Contest
Award Winning Poetry
2007

Unequal by Julinar Diab
2007 IWA Member Category Winner

We're living in a dark age
With luxuries galore
Things are just the same
As the centuries before

Yet now comes a new twist
Electric eyes and ears
Watching and recording
Their subjects far and near

Kings still exploit the poor
And take away the land
Torture any peasant
Who tries to take a stand

Now dressed in suits and ties
They tell us that we're free
And its the flock of doves
Who threaten liberty

They rob people of their minds
And most degradingly
All based on their belief
And spirituality

Don't mention untold truths
Don't mention muted youths
Or wartime trauma diaries
How could they start anew?

Man was created weak
Can perform good or evil
Without true guidance
Is worse than any devil

We're living in a dark age
With luxuries galore
Things are just the same
As the centuries before

Yet now comes a new twist
Electric eyes and ears
Watching and recording
Their subjects far and near

Kings still exploit the poor
And take away the land
Torture any peasant
Who tries to take a stand

Now dressed in suits and ties
They tell us we're not free
Yes, it's the flock of doves
Despising democracy?

They rob people of their rights
And human dignity
Based on the garments they adorn
And nationality

Don't mention slavery
Don't mention equality
Or child laborers
Whose tears could fill the sea

Man was created weak
Can perform good or evil
Without true guidance
Is worse than any devil

Julinar Diab AKA Sister Um Ibrahim is the mother of six children and recently moved to the Gulf with husband and family. Um Ibrahim has been writing poetry and short stories for over 20 years. She enjoys spending time with her family and friends. She has been drawing since the age of two and loves nature. She is a member of the professional Muslim organization, Islamic Writers Alliance.

MANY THANKS TO OUR JUDGES

Youth Judge: Noura Durkee, author, *Yunus & the Whale* and others

IWA Member Judge and Adult Judge: Dasham Brookins, Muslim Poet.com

Islamic Writers Alliance
4th Annual Poetry Contest
Member Award Winning Poem
2008

A Haiku - Sequence by Camilla Sayf
2008 IWA Member Category Winner

nourishing sounds
of the Holy Koran's verse
dry leaves fade away

strain against evil
recite prayer most steadfast
captured in snow storm

give your soul to Rabb
amid blossoming gardens
blissful revival

cheerful green burst out
shouting all names of Allah
submission's the key

Camilla Sayf is a haiku poet, freelance writer, and the author of "Lebanese Chronicles." She is a former language teacher who finds her conversion to Islam to be her greatest inspiration. Her work has been published in MuslimHeritage.com, Qalam, MuslimWakeUp, DaralislamLive, and Breakthrough. Some of her writings, including "Lebanese Chronicles" and "Innocent Heart," have been translated & published in other languages.

Public Judging of Poetry Entries

The 2008 IWA Poetry Contest was judged by a Public Vote.
The poem receiving the most votes was determined
as the winning poem.

Islamic Writers Alliance
5th Annual Poetry Contest
Member Award Winning Poem
2009

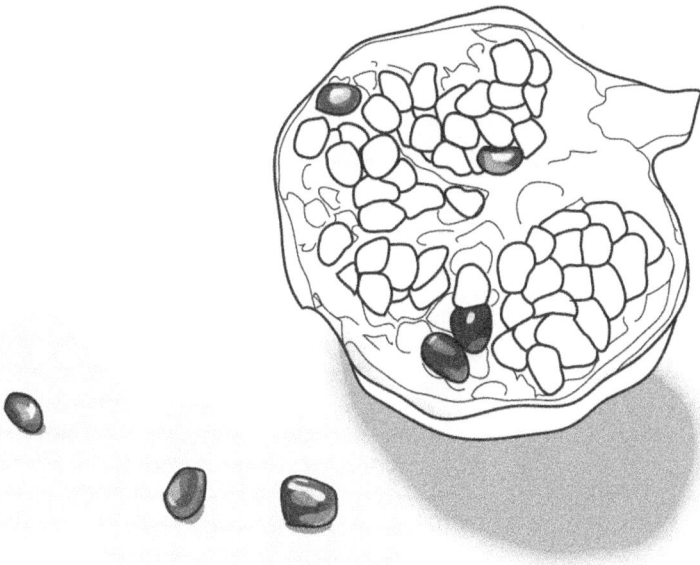

The Key by - Marwa Elnaggar
2009 IWA Member Category Winner

It waits at the bottom of a trunk
At the bottom of a drawer, it waits.
It grows old, it grows old
Passing from hand to hand
From gnarled hands that unfold
Faded cloth to unveil history
To destined hands of grandchildren,
The generation in between, lost
Lies waiting
Under the earth.

Different foods, different smells
Waft through distant kitchens
The walls of the houses are hearing
Different words, different laughter.
The joys and sorrows are unlike
Those of old, that lie waiting
Behind memories.

Just-for-now lives lived
In just-for-now houses
Stay warm with inherited stories.
The dreams of old grow cold
As just-for-now turns from weeks
To months to years
And a century of just-for-now
Lies waiting
Around the corner of history books.

Different hands open the windows every morning
Different feet walk upon the floors
Different eyes look out on the horizon
In the distance.

In the distance, eyes that have grown old
With waiting, gaze back,
Seeing a distant gleaming dome of gold,
Seeing beyond the borders
Beyond the distance
Beyond the history,
Windows and kitchens and floors
That once were familiar,
Seeing the doors of Palestine
Waiting
For the old familiar keys.

Marwa Elnaggar is an Egyptian writer, poet, critic, and media consultant. She has traveled extensively throughout Africa, Asia, Europe, and the US. Her interests include storytelling, arts & crafts, painting, nature, music, and photography. She holds an MA in English and Comparative Literature from the American University in Cairo. She received her BA in English Literature (Hons) from the University of Delhi in India. She has been studying Islam in Cairo, Egypt since 2001. You can contact her at marwa.writing@gmail.com.

Many Thanks to Our Judges

Youth Judge: Karen English, author, *Nadia's Hands*

Adult Judge: Dasham Brookins, Muslim Poet.com

IWA Member Judge: Daniel Abdal-Hayy Moore
http://www.danielmoorepoetry.com/

Islamic Writers Alliance
IWA Members Poems
2009

In Loving Remembrance of Amatullah Al-Marwani
A Smile
The Passion of the Muslim

A Smile by Amatullah Al-Marwani

A smile of great breadth and warmth graces my face today.
With friends like this, who needs a vacation get-away?

I can bask in your humor, tan in the brilliance of your mirth.
I might dish it out, but you give it to me for all you're worth!

When complain I do, venting often and out loud,
My words pass over, a floating, unbothered cloud.

And when I try to storm, thunder and hail upon the land
You sit back and press the delete key with a steady hand.

How can I get on top, beat this crowd of jackette be nimbles?
You're stuck to me like glue, through all my quirks and quimbles.

(Okay, that wasn't a real word but give me some leeway
My fingers are racing faster than cars on the Indy speedway)

And to close this little jaunt into my world of rhyme,
I'll say this (can't say it enough) again, one more time…

Though here we laugh, and cry, and spill out our beans
Having friends like all of you is wealth beyond my means.

And I'll have to finish here because I've lost my rhyming touch.
:sigh: Being grown up and doing grown up stuff sure hurts much!

But serving Allah, whether as Tulip or Pammie or Linda or Jane
Makes me thankful He took me away from the ordinary and plain.

The next time you smile, have one on me.
I'll be smiling twice because you're so darn fun-ny!

THE PASSION OF THE MUSLIM BY AMATULLAH AL-MARWANI

This is one movie you have absolutely got to see,
Says the Christian to the Muslim with joyful glee.

It's all about Jesus Christ, your Lord and Savior Most High!
It's all about seeing him ripped to shreds and then watching him die!

But, but, thinks the Muslim, bewildered at the movie's plot.
Doesn't Allah say in the Holy Qur'an, "And they Killed him not!"?

Maybe so, maybe so, invites the Christian, not caring a whit.
We'll just sit together and watch your confusion fade in a little bit.

Besides, what's the harm? It's only a movie show!
(But, they hide the truth because they really do know...)

(They know once you've seen, you can never unsee;
Once you are bound to falsehood, it's hard to break free...)

(They know once a foot is in the door, the other will follow;
All the weak protesting will become void, null and hollow...)

(They know their job is to bring the Muslim in closer;
The rest is up to the movie's director and composer...)

(They know the tricks of the trade plied by Hollywood so well:
Music, lights, camera, action—even lies become an easy sell...)

(They know the seed of doubt will be buried in fertile soil;
it'll grow and sprout someday even without much toil...)

(They know once you've heard you can never unhear;
ideas become cloudy that were once perfectly clear...)

(They know their truth can become yours, too;
only the price of a ticket, popcorn, and maybe a Mountain Dew...)

(They know one last argument will help with the fight…
"Hey, I heard they blame the Jews! Isn't that right?!")

Thinking it over, the Muslim will finally decide
It's okay to go because I'm strong on the inside.

Nothing will get me to shun what I believe is true.
Nothing will get me to do what I know I should not do.

But, I don't really want to go on my lonesome on my own
Let me bring Ahmad and Basheer into the danger zone.

So now the Muslim invites Muslim with joyful glee
This is one movie you absolutely must see!

Anxious hands pay the twenty bucks to get in.
Who ever said there wasn't a cost to sin?

In the dark, men and women together side by side
Sit silent as Jesus Christ was tortured and died.

Not a one stands tall, calls out, makes a loud cry.
"This is not the truth! The Prophet of God did not die!"

Not a one enjoins the good and forbids the wrong
They sit in silent acceptance, a follower of the throng.

Each finds reason, excuse, cause to stay.
"I've got to warn others to keep away!"

"I've got to make sure I can fight this untruth!"
"I've got to understand so I can advise our youth!"

I've got to do this and that and the other thing, too.
I've got reasons for the dunya. But for the akhira, too?

"What would Jesus do?" the Christians often ask.
Finding an answer for a Muslim isn't a difficult task.

He'd proclaim to one and all as he did before:
Believe in Allah. Heed the warning. Do not ignore.

Use your twenty bucks to support a good cause.
Buy heaven, not hell! Don't act without pause!

Rise up and deliver my message wise and straight
Oh, Muslim, invite all to our way, don't sit by and wait!

This movie can lead to the straight and perfect path.
It's an open door for Muslims to avoid Allah's wrath.

Don't walk through to dark seats lined up in a neat row.
Lead the people with the Words you are blessed to know.

O, Son of Mary, Jesus Christ, anointed, high in rank.
Beloved Messenger of Allah, it's Him we praise and thank.

The film will fade, excitement will wane as the furor slips away.
But the Muslims won't forget what happened to Jesus that day.

We don't need Hollywood to guide our light
We have ISLAM to teach us wrong ... from RIGHT.

© 2004 Amatullah Al-Marwani

Amatullah Al-Marwani (*penned herself The Mad Rhyming Woman*) was one of the founding members of the IWA organization. She was married to Mohamed and the mother of a son, Zaahir, and a daughter, Amirah. Sister Amatullah authored the *Zaahir and the Camel* children's book series, wrote extensive poetry, created newsletters for her masjid and community, and served Allah with a heart full of love. She died April 29, 2005 from leukemia. I was honored to be her writing buddy for over four years, and she was my dearest friend. For those she left behind, her work is still a great pleasure to read and learn from.

—*Linda Delgado AKA Widad*

Tahira Abdul Jalil
A Convert's Tale

He went into his garden in a state of mind unjust to his soul:
He said, "I deem not that this will ever perish (Quran 18:35)

The earth that nurtured me is covered
With new condos and townhouses—
It is gone beneath fresh sidewalks and sod

Those who live here now
Do not touch the earth

The earth that felt the pounding
Of children's playful feet as they ran and shrieked
And laughed through childhood games
In front of ancient apartments where no one
Was poor (for how can you be poor if you
Have what everyone else has?)—
Where there were only the aunts and uncles and cousins
The grandparents, the neighbors, the churchgoers
The shopkeepers who'd known my people
For thirty years or more
That earth was my refuge

Those who drive past manicured lawns
In quiet, air-conditioned cars do not hear the earth

The earth that heard the sounds
Of lovemaking, of arguments and fights
Of the grown-ups who left each day
To struggle through a racial world outside
Then came back to bury their frustrations,
Their pain and their humiliations in gin and sin and sex,
In parties and in music and in joy
Of small brown babies that toddled among them

Those who relish smooth white walls, new stone edifices
And fresh concrete do not see the earth

The earth that saw generations
Scattered and displaced as bulldozers destroyed
And wrecking crews eviscerated their memory
From the landscape
Or the building crews that came to construct
Other lives heedless of those
Whose blood and tears and joy
Were now locked in the earth beneath their feet

I see them unaware and remember
How as a child in this same place
I tried to listen for the sounds
Of forests that I knew had been there once,
And pretended I could almost hear the lives
In the Odawa villages trapped beneath my sidewalks

Now Allah has blessed me
To understand His meaning
Through the memory of my life
As it rests beneath my own feet
Buried below the newly paved streets
And lost somewhere in the earth

Tahira Abdul-Jalil converted to Islam in 1974 and made Hajj in 1982. She writes for both children and adults. For children, she prefers to write stories in rhyme that teach about having a strong Muslim character. Her adult themes are expressed in poetry and in vignettes about Muslims who are struggling to find, to strengthen, or to return to their faith in an increasingly secular world.

She has co-authored several articles in the forthcoming *Encyclopedia of Muslim-American History*, Edward E. Curtis IV, editor. She blogs at www.muslimwritings.com. She also writes for www.footstepstohajj. com, the blog for *Footsteps to Paradise*, an organization that helps Muslims make Hajj.

She has friends who are Sunni, Sufi, and Shia. She wants very much to make Hajj again. This is her first published story.

Rym Aoudia
A Living Faith

i breathed into a jar
perhaps i could see my soul
and know which shape
this faith would take
so i could clutch it
and never ever lose it

'It's there'

inside my heart i searched
feeling around with my hands
careful not to block the arteries
and exclamations in between
then in my brain i did the same
feeling my way through the folds
and question marks within

'It's there'

perhaps i should search for belief
if found, then faith should be near
somewhere in my reason and feelings
i could find their tracks
and understand
so my mouth won't utter a noise
of contradictions, of confusions

perhaps i should look behind me
what my tracks have left behind
faith might be in my treaded path
taking the form of actions
beyond uttered words and sentiments

'Aah, it's there'

listen with me
my human nature speaking

voiced like a breeze
a universal language
time is now fluid, dimensions now a mirage
what i barely noticed
is stepping into my vision
tapping into my innate fuel
a supply of faith
driving my path

with those pendulum thoughts
the night rocked me to sleep

and with those same thoughts
dawn lifted my eyelids

see it with me
splendors of early morning
changing hues, varying tunes
energy rising beneath the darkness
welcoming the break of dawn
crawling, walking, flying creatures
celebrating the new day
there was passion

I bow down in praise

there it was
all around me, beyond my 'i'
energy so vast, in many forms
a faith beheld
the fuel of life

Rym Aoudia - Sister Rym has been an IWA member since the time the organization was founded. She presently resides in the Middle East. She is a well-known comic strip writer and illustrator. Her political comic strips have been published in several leading UK magazines and online Muslim web sites, notably IslamOnline.net.

SAALEHA BHAMJEE

GREY
A FAMILY AFFAIR
HIS PAINTING
UMMATI

GREY BY SAALEHA BHAMJEE

Grass dormant, in death like sleep
crunchy beneath her weakened feet
as she drags her tired shadow
on the path that grows ever narrow

each day the same, effete
a lurid picture, ghostly grey
the colour of each remaining day
was there a time when they were…more?

bright, alive, burning with possibility
a blank canvas to be filled with
tastes, textures and living
yes living….would that she could

yet she filled it with regret
and more regret again
sorrow about what was
anger at what was not

she filled it with hate and greed
jealousy and simple misery
the colours that spilled
were reds, only reds – like blood

the blood of hate, and anger

her trees have long since borne fruit
her fruit have thorns, she cannot bear them
thorns that are children with loud voices
children who trample on her brown grass

the reds have faded – green at first
growing more grey with each passing day
her canvas is ruined – the work of her own hand
her shadow, like her soul – tired, worn, grey

A Family Affair by Saaleha Bhamjee

Look at us
We're all we have
Yet peace and joy
Have eluded us

We're family? say you
What family? say I
You go your way
And I go mine
Paths separated
Never to intertwine

Over things mundane
And statements inane
Do we quarrel and bicker
While loving each other
Would be that much quicker
Or perhaps it'd be too great a bother

Yet, for T.V. and mall-hopping
Trips to the park and picnicking,
Annual holidays at the coast,
Time for these do we boast
Yet for family, this is much to ask
Seemingly too difficult a task

Our parents' wealth has brought this day?
Yet somehow it seems, it's always been this way
We'd gather at Eid but always a-grumbling
I've done too much, you'd find us mumbling
Snide remarks would be the order of the day
Could we not have found something better to say?

We'll cry at one another's funerals, we will
He'd better be certain I'm mentioned in his will
To his grave did I carry him with my own hand
Then cover him with a ton of sand
Perhaps for him, did I not pray
But he did plenty preparing for this day

It was the same when our parents died
Truly, how each one of us cried
Sincere tears, really they were
As sincere as mummy's were
When there was none to listen to her fears
When there was none to ease the burden of her years

And Daddy spent the last years of his life alone
Moving miserably from home to home
While his daughters-in-law moaned about his ways
Begrudging him happiness in his final days
And when he died, joyfully they cried
We'll miss him dearly, they lied

Then greedily their bags they filled
Around his belongings they milled
Stealing the choicest of his goods
Fighting over his antique woods
Claiming back gifts they gave
These no one else could have

So now Eid has become a solitary affair
Everyone apparently too busy to care
My own family, that's all that matters
So who needs sisters or brothers?
When I am old, care for me, my children will
Like I did for mummy and daddy when they were ill

His Painting by Saaleha Bhamjee

I caught a glimpse of Him the other day. Of His hands as they – paint drenched – dragged their way across the western sky. Broad expansive strokes. His colours were of peaches – a gentle yellow; apricots – tantalisingly close to orange; blood red pomegranates; even lavender. He sprayed the clouds a grey until they became bluish mountains against a whitening sky.

But there was something wrong. He was crying. His tears fell onto the canvas and blended the colours, bled them into one another, forced them to meld, to mix, to become one. A solid mass of swirling hue. When last had I seem Him paint like this?

Perhaps He cried for the orphan child, living on the street and sniffing glue to forget his troubles. Or for the young girl who would play wife to her father, or another. Perhaps He cried for the boy with gnawing innards who picks through the garbage of a family bloated by excess. Perhaps He cries for my forgetfulness, my arrogance, my heedlessness.

But even with His tears, He creates such a picture, such breathtaking beauty that for a single instant, the picture comes sharply into focus. For a single instant, I see Him, and I know that I will always be His.

True Love

To love until you feel like dying
to wring from your soul every last tear
to pray for the last day just to see His face
to beg for Paradise only to bow at His feet

Have you felt it?

The joy, yet misery
of love that consumes
and yearning that devours
and despair that destroys

Have you known it?

You speak of love
yet you give preference
to the selfish dictates
of your avaricious soul

You speak of faith
yet you engross yourself
in fears of tomorrow
and concerns of yesterday

You speak of mercy
yet you've done nothing
to earn that gift
or any other

You speak of forgiveness
yet you've never repented
until you wished to tear
out your own eyes
to stop the tears

You claim to know Him
How can you?
when you know not yourself

UMMATI BY SAALEHA BHAMJEE

In every sacred deed
In every sacred step
In every sacred word
And every sacred breath
Ummati is infused
Ummati pervades
Ummati dominates
Ummati determines
From the very first day
To the bloody shoes of Taif
To the lost teeth of Uhud
To the very last breath
To the plains of Hashr
Ummati, Ummati
The cries of the soul
Troubled
In blissful agony
Of obedience
Yet Ummati flounders
Ummati blunders
Ummati forgets
Ummati ignores
Forgets the pain
Of the stones at Taif
The spears of Uhud
The agonies of death
The dread of Hashr
Ummati
Ummati
A cry in the wilderness
Of stony hearts
And greedy souls
Ummati
Ummati

Saaleha Bhamjee began her writing career as a columnist for the South African print magazine, *The Muslim Woman*. Her writings have appeared on Islam Online, An Nisaa magazine, *The Straight Path Magazine*, *Al Qalam* newspaper, the New Orleans-based *Iqra*, as well as the UK-based *Muslim Weekly*. She has had poems appear in the *Muslim Voices Anthology 2006*.She worked as a reviewer for the Islamic Poetry website and was a judge in their Praise the Prophet Competition. Her first book, *The Beautiful Names*, has been published by Muslim Writers Publishing. It is available online and is due for release in South Africa in 2009. She is working on a few novels and has completed a collection of short stories, which she hopes to have published. A few of these stories appear on the prestigious South African literary website, LitNet. She blogs sporadically on http://afrocentric-muslimah.blogspot.com/, which serves as a showcase of sorts for her writing. Saaleha is a member of the Islamic Writers Alliance and is also the owner of Lazeeza's Bakery and Confectionery.

Brandy AZ Chase

Women's Silent Tears
Pray One
Child's Jannah

Women's Silent Tears by Brandy AZ Chase

How many tears have been shed,

because of few words said,
by voices low and deep,

How many more must weep,
withhold them, they cannot keep,
down faces very pale,

Through grief; the silent wail,
battling emotions, they fail,
yet inside they harden,

Though they beg for pardon,
hearts locked up by wardens,
who really has the key?

Lioness all will see,
selflessly, protects her family,
yet inside a mouse,

Rocking numbly in her house,
always pining for her spouse,
those escaping little tears,

Exposing all her fears,
subjecting her to jeers,
but her soul's strong,

Though they do her wrong,
she'll bite her willing tongue,
bottled in her head.

Many more tears shed,
ringing her eyes with dread,
underneath they simmer,

Resolving with a glimmer,
blurring smiles with a shimmer,
they fall without sound,

Fresh throughout the rounds,
pacing the same ground,
so soft she was Made,

But, she must stand brave,
Allah's mercy does she crave,
Women's silent tears.

Pray One by Brandy AZ Chase

Crowded city streets
Untold financial feats,
I bow my head down
Forehead touching ground
I pray on.

Their eyes question
What's my intention,
I close my eyes; recite
With all my might
I pray on.

Pass by snickering
Certain finger flickering,
I bend like a V
Hands on my knees
I pray on.

Loud dancing beat
Lyrics so sweet,
I put my finger up
Shahada, no disrupt
I pray on.

Smell burger & fries
At bottom of high rise,
I feel Allah's stare
Watching me with care
I pray on.

Always,
I pray on.

CHILD'S JANNAH by BRANDY AZ CHASE

There must be lots of treats
Like candies and sweets.
Castles to explore
Adventure around every door.
Flowers so big and red
Sleeping on them like a bed.
Singing all day long
A forever happy song.
Rivers of milk and honey,
Houses that shine like money.
Mommy and Daddy together,
No more bad weather.
No more loud yelling
Or Brother and Sister telling.
Eating crumbly cakes
While jumping on beds as big as lakes.
Glitter everywhere
Even in my hair.
Clouds of cream filling,
Within my reach, are milling.
Flying up high
In the rainbow colored sky.
Best of all I love dearly,
Seeing Allah clearly.

Brandy AZ Chase was born and raised in sunny Tucson, Arizona, USA. She converted to Islam at seventeen from Atheism and goes by the Islamic name of Aminah-Zahira. She lived in Lebanon for four years before moving to Al-Ain, United Arab Emirates, where she currently resides with her Lebanese husband and two children.

She has been writing poetry, sci-fi, fantasy, romance, and historical novels since she was twelve. Also she has been studying art and drawing with different mediums. Recently discovering the genre of Islamic Fiction, she has written many short stories and poems. In addition to writing, she does home schooling, art work, interior and landscape designing, and blogging at http://www.brandyachase.blogspot.com/.

She created an All Muslimah Blog Directory at http://www.allmuslimah.blogspot.com/ and can be reached through her e-mail BrandyAZChase@gmail.com.

Of the things in life she loves are books, sword fighting, wooden ships, tiger lilies, delving into the realms of Imagination, and above all Allah and all the great things Islam has brought to her life.

Ginger Davis
The Search

Truth,
Hiding under the branches of a tree called assumption.
Wearing the mask of gold and jewels called culture.
Lost in the words of an old book called tradition.

Truth,
Like a fire, we are drawn to its warmth
A stream of pure water and we are thirsty travelers
The peace of rituals when we are souls under siege.

Truth,
Forever unspoken,
Always obscured,
Never waiting to be discovered.
And yet we are searching for it
Bowing in houses of worship,
Hoping it will be there when we lift our heads.

Books and scholars hovering over it,
Like flies drawn to summer's fruit

It is Him.
And we will never know it,
Never taste it,
Never feel it,
Never wrap it around our bodies like a warm quilt in the winter.

We leave this life hungry for it,
Just the way we entered it.

The reason for this life behind veils unknown,
To even the greatest thinkers.

Maybe the only truth is simply that there is no truth,
Our search is not for truth.
Our emptiness not for that unattainable knowledge.

Our search is not for truth, but for the Divine.

Ginger Davis is a Muslim American and mother to four wonderful children living in Wyoming. She is also a lifelong reader and writer. She majored in English at Chapman University in California. Currently she is blogging and aspiring to finish her first novel. Read more about her at www.ummlayla.blogspot.com.

LINDA D. DELGADO
HE'S COMING!
WHO WILL STANDUP FOR ME?
COME WALK WITH ME, COME TALK WITH ME
*MY HERO IS YOUR HERO

HE'S COMING! BY LINDA D. DELGADO

Two hours late
Dinner is cold, now
Door slams with a BANG
Mama whispers, Hurry Miriam!
Hide!

Fear

In my closet
Inside the toy box. Close the lid
He's shouting at Mama
Glass and furniture breaking
Mama screams and screams.

Terror

I cover my ears
My eyes tightly squeezed shut
Waiting...terrified!
Afraid to breathe
Heavy footsteps in my room.

Silence

Mama's not crying, now
Footsteps going away
How long to stay hidden?
Silent tears fall
Poor mama. Quiet...wait for mama.

Fitful sleep

Awake. I'm frightened
Loud voices calling
Miriam? Miriam? Calling my name
But not Mama's voice
Heavy footsteps getting closer. He's coming!
He's coming!

I scream and scream
Sisters from the masjid look down at me
Where's my mama?
We'll take care of you, they say
We're here to help you.

Like you helped my mama?
She begged for help
You turned your faces away
It's not my problem
All of you would say.

Go away

I want my mama! I scream
But I know by the look on their faces
Hush Miriam, your Mama's gone
He won't hurt her again
How can he...I wail. She's dead!

I scream and scream.

Who Will Standup For Me? by Linda D. Delgado

Waiting…

She huddled on the floor
Ahmed glared at her from the open door.
Amina looked at him in abject fear.
She knew better than to cry a tear.

Her heart thudded wildly, her chest filled with pain.
He shouted words cruel and profane.
She lifted her eyes…watched him draw near.
The man she had loved who had once called her dear.

Cringing…

Not one more word from you.
You know very well what I can do.
He snatched the head scarf off her head.
And threw it down on the broken bed.

While I am gone you will not move.
Else more than a head scarf will you lose.
It's all your fault and I don't care
Stupid woman you have made me late for prayer.

With that said he stormed out of the house.
Muttering he did not deserve such a spouse.
Amina crawled to the bedside chair
Her busted lip dripping blood everywhere

I Will Stand Up For You…

Amina? Amina! What has happened to you?
Her neighbor Yasmin paused then said I know what to do.
Amina's quavering voice replied I am okay.
Don't worry…no need for you to stay.

Nonsense, you are coming with me
I am taking you to a safe place, you will see.
Don't argue and do not feel dread
My husband Tarek will handle Ahmed.

Yasmin and Amina sat quietly behind the screen
In the prayer room they could not be seen.
Amina's sisters whispered to her softly
We stand up for you. Stand up with me.

Friday Kutbah ended and Imam said brothers don't go
I have a matter you all must know
He pointed to Ahmed and said it is time to stop your harm
You cannot hide your wrong behind your charm.

Tarek stood next to the Imam for all to see
I stand up for Sister Amina. Who will stand up for her with me?
One by one the brothers stood
Brothers in union said we stand up as we should.

COME WALK WITH ME. COME TALK WITH ME
BY LINDA D. DELGADO

I stood silently among the crowd
Uncomfortable, yet unwilling to break free
Each stranger wore the cloak of sin
Their foul smell seeping into me.
My eyes darted here and there
I sensed someone beckoning to me
and my heart yearned when I saw him
Standing upon a lighted straight and narrow path
His words wafted on the breeze
Come walk with me. Come talk with me.

My heart swelled, as my footsteps drew me towards him
But then, I stumbled, doubted, and turned my face away
For just a second
When I looked back my panic rose
Where is he? Where did the lighted path go?
Instead to my right and to my left
Only crooked, dark, and lonely paths
I raced down each with evil laughter following me
Dark, cold, foul-smelling places ending in an Abyss
Panic. Awareness of my loss growing steadily

He was nowhere to be found
Not in these places. Only the strangers in that crowd
Falling to my knees. Tears streaming from my eyes
All my wrong doings spilling from my lips
I cried aloud: O Allah where did he go?
Alone now and frightened. Quiet descends
The silence is broken by that gentle breeze
And then once more I hear him calling to me
Come walk with me. Come talk with me.
There he is! Beloved Prophet of Islam!
Now I accept him, most praiseworthy guide,
Now, I am a Muslim, Now I am free.

*My Hero Is Your Hero by Linda D. Delgado

We sat around the table, my daughter, son, and me.
Shall I tell you a new story?
They both chorused, No! Let me. Let me.
Hmm...I responded. Let's play a guessing game instead.
We'll take turns describing favorite heroes
And then guess who they could be.

My hero was a great leader and fought bravely in each battle.
My hero washed his clothes with no complaint and was kind to
    all he met.
What a coincidence, I said, because my hero did both of these...
Son said his hero was the greatest teacher the world had ever
    known.
Daughter giggled and said her hero and his wife played racing
    games.
How amazing, I exclaimed, because my hero did both of these.

A dark cloud in the sky followed my hero when he was just a boy.
Daughter claimed her hero became a great trader while working
    for his wife.
Oh, my! This is astounding because my hero did both of these.
Son scratched his head while thinking hard. Not willing to give
    up.
Daughter twirled her braid and thought aloud, who can Mom's
    hero be?
I smiled knowingly at both of them and waited patiently.

Son grinned broadly and then announced importantly
My hero never told a lie and taught Muslims how to pray.
Daughter said her hero could top that. Son said there was no way.
My hero talked to Allah's Angel, she declared dramatically.
My goodness, I said with wonder, because my hero did both of
    these!
At this point my children protested. You haven't told us anything!

So I declared my hero left his Sunnah for all mankind to
    understand.
He recited each of Allah's Words in our most honored Qur'an.
I know! I know! Both clamored wildly, waving hands at me.
Your hero is our hero, they exclaimed excitedly.
They had solved the guessing game and were bursting with their
    glee.
Our hero is the Last Prophet, Muhammad, the most Trusted and
    Praiseworthy.

American Poet Takes Top Adult Prize in
Prophet Mohammad Poetry Contest

The winners of the first annual Praise the Prophet International Poetry Competition were announced online at http://www.islamicpoetry. com. The top prize in the adult category went to Linda Delgado of Tempe, Arizona, for her submission titled *My Hero Is Your Hero*.

Linda D. Delgado is a mother, grandmother, and great grandmother. She graduated from the University of Phoenix and is a retired Arizona DPS Sergeant. Linda is the author of the award-winning children's book series, Islamic Rose Books, *Grandma & Hijab Family Activity Book*, and two non-fiction books: *Halal Food, Fun and Laughter* and *A Muslim's Guide to Publishing and Marketing*. Linda is also the creator of the Grandma & Hijab-Ez comic strip series and the owner-publisher of *Muslim Writers Publishing*,: a traditional Muslim publishing house in its fourth year with twenty titles published. www. MuslimWritersPublishing.com and www.widad-lld.com

Julinar Diab

A Merciful Gift
The Reality

A Merciful Gift by Julinar Diab

How can I explain with my limited knowledge
All the beauty and honor which adorned our Prophet
May the peace and eternal blessings be upon him
He was a light in the darkness yet some couldn't see it
Shine
They couldn't feel the warmth
They couldn't hear the peace
Hearts were too hard
Almighty God's decree
Wishing I had witnessed the grace, and sweet smiling face
Bright as the silver sun-lit moon, with every sin erased
May the goodness and eternal bounties be upon him
He was a symbol of love yet some wouldn't feel it
Glow
They wouldn't grasp its heat
They wouldn't silence fear
Some did not believe
The Glorious Truth sent clear
How could I ever live without the Final Prophet
And the embracing, healing wisdom he was sent with
May all the guidance and eternal protection be upon him
He was chosen by God yet his people rejected Him
May we be united soon
After our trial starts
That we might be the chosen few
To be given a sinless heart
Just as the Messenger of Allah, a humble, devoted servant
His heart was washed by Angels from the spring God sent
Noble, just, wise, pious, full of love ever strong
A merciful gift, his Sunnah we rely on

Now
Like it was back then
Forever protected
Until time ends
And our true life begins

THE REALITY BY JULINAR DIAB

Don't they see, the miracles of life?
To see something come from nothing!
And their own hands, are paralyzed
They don't recognize the owner of such things.

They deny the truth, from their Lord
While He has created the world around them
And how perfectly He fashions their forms
Can't they see His creatures in submission?

Everything points to the oneness of Allah
Yet they don't acknowledge sign after sign
And they're so eager to set up rivals
How arrogant and ungrateful is mankind?

They consume with greed, the blessings and bounties
Allah ta'ala has spread out before them
And with hearts so hard and eyes too blind to see
The reality – He's Allah, our final destination.

Julinar Diab AKA Sister Um Ibrahim is the mother of six children and recently moved to the Gulf with husband and family. Um Ibrahim has been writing poetry and short stories for over 20 years. She enjoys spending time with her family and friends. She has been drawing since the age of two and loves nature. She is a member of the professional Muslim organization, Islamic Writers Alliance.

JUDY NELSON ELDAWY

MY HOPE
WORDS

MY HOPE BY JUDY NELSON ELDAWY

My tiny little miracle.
I loved you before your heart began to beat.
I dreamed of holding you in my arms
While singing you to sleep.
But then my hopes shattered
Washed away in a river of red.
Now the flood of tears
Flashing thru my soul
Leave it barren as my womb.
inshaallah...InshaAllah... INSHA-ALLAH !
Both become fertile again.

WORDS BY JUDY NELSON-ELDAWY

Words – ahhh words,
like the blood in my veins
They course thru my brain
They trickle and slide
like the water down drains
goes to nourish the corn
that grows on the plains
These words – such words
germinate in my brain
nourishing ideas
both good and profane
which lie fallow like seeds
awaiting the rains
These words – my words
gestate in my brain
They grow and they swell

til frustrated and struggling
with laboring pains
They burst free
giving birth to my work
Offspring of my brain
Words, ahhh…words…

Judy Nelson Eldawy or Ummcamelia winters in Egypt and, with her daughter and husband, spends summers in USA. Judy earned a BSN from George Mason University.

Judy writes, "I remember my Mom saying I should be a writer when I was little, but I wanted to be an anthropologist and an archeologist. Then reality reared its ugly head, and I became an RN, mostly because housing and groceries are two of my favorite things. Alhumdulilah as I turned out to love nursing. I have worked with HIV/AIDS patients, in medical/surgical, psychological/mental health and home health.

"I married and ended up moving to and migrating between Small Town, USA and Small Village, Egypt. Allah Alim-Margaret Mead of the Delta fellaheen, that's me. I try to maintain a serene and tranquil home for my darlings in both places. In between tutoring and domestic engineering, I surf the Web, read, and research – especially herbal medicines and alternative treatments – and do some freelance writing."

YAHIYA EMERICK

THE NIGHTMARE
THE WOODLANDERS

THE NIGHTMARE by YAHIYA EMERICK

I dreamt a dream,
A dream of doom.
I dreamt I fell
Within a tomb!

Not four close walls
Did I espy,
But a long cathedral
And pillars by

A guard of bones,
A skeletal troop,
Rushed forth to seize me
Within their loop.

Before their altar
Was I drug,
A stone affair
'Round a pit, well-dug.

A call rang forth
And fast as that,
A flame Emerged
Atop the flat.

A basin near
Then filled with goo.
An oozy slime
Like day-old gruel.

In fear and dread
Did I perspire,
For the bone men brought me
Near the fire.

"Who," it boomed,
"Doth dare inquire?"
"Who," it loomed,
"Doth stoke my fire?"

"Not me," said I
in such a haste,
Not wishing the flame
Of me to taste.

Then a raging clamor
Did start to happen.
The floor and the ceiling
Shook with a clappin'.

The walls of the tomb
Did shift and shake.
And the bone men shattered
In its wake.

The darkness cleared
And haze alightened.
Then I woke up in my bed –
Alone and Frightened.

The Woodlanders by Yahiya Emerick

Never knew much of wood or ferry,
Thought nothing of briar, bramble or huckleberry,
Forests were dark and fields fool's gold,
Deep places where nobody goes.

But on a whim I took a stroll,
And entered in where nature grows,
Fear and unease soon dispelled,
And a love of trees soon befell.

O Grace of God on this wood unfold!
I've loved this place many times untold.
When winter's hand doth lay her wreath,
And clothes thee in her snowy sleep,
Till eve of spring doth melt thy heart,
And beckons for thy life to start.

Ever and anon remains,
My heart with thee,
Till ends my days.

Yahiya Emerick is a convert to Islam who has worked to bridge the gap between traditional knowledge and modern needs. He has authored 25 books on Islam directed towards students, converts, and the wider interfaith community. His recently completed translation of the Holy Qur'an into modern English is widely anticipated and is designed to fill the needs of both Muslims and non-Muslims in understanding the historical context of the revelation. He has also been an active speaker and promoter of Islamic values.

Fawzia Gilani
Twas the Night Before Eid (Adapted)

Twas the night before Eid,
When all through the house,
Everyone was excited,
Even the mouse,
New clothes were hung,
In the closet with care,
In the hopes that Eid,
Would soon be there.
The children were nestled,
All snug in their beds,
While visions of kulfi
Appeared in their heads.
When out on the lawn,
There arose such a clatter,
I sprang from the bed,
To see what was the matter,
Away to the window,
I flew in a flash
Tore open the shutters,
And threw up the sash.
The moon a slight crest,
Up in the sky,
Twinkled against the minaret high,
When what to my wondering
Eyes should appear,
But an orphan boy cowering with fear.
Forgive me brother,
He called to me,
I slipped and fell,
I did not see,
I have walked through the mountains,
I've come a long way,
I was told it was Eid,
On this fine blessed day.

You are right, my boy,
I said to him,
Please enter our home and rest within.
The poor boy's clothes were covered with dirt.
Bruises and scratches all told where he hurt.
I'm from a town,
In a land far away,
Said the boy with tears,
I've no place to stay.
My heart felt sad,
As I looked at him,
He was so young,
So very thin.

Ama arose and told him to wait,
She gave him clean clothes,
And cried at his fate,
With us you will stay,
She whispered to him
Laying her hand
On his scratched up chin.
And so on Eid day
We gave him some toys,
But he spent his time sitting,
Making no noise,
He thought of his mother,
His home and his brother,
He thought of his town,
His kin and other.
Tis the day of Eid,
A day of joy and care,
Please sit beside us,
Be welcome and share.
But the orphan was sad,
Filled with grief,
There was nothing
We could say to bring him relief.

And then there came a knock at the door,
The orphan's gaze lifted up from the floor.
A smile appeared as his eyes filled with tears,
The face before him,
He'd not seen for years,
The young man came was his older brother,
Who gathered him up with the embrace of a mother.
I have come for you from far, far away,
He said to him for this blessed Eid day!

*Kulfi – a type of Indian ice-cream.

Fawzia Gilani is the author of more than twenty children's books. She was born and raised in Walsall, England. Her passion is children's Islamic literature, which she is studying at the University of Worcester, UK. She has worked as a teacher since 1993 and as a librarian since 2005. She currently works as the principal of An-Noor Private School in Windsor, Ontario. She makes her home in Oberlin, Ohio, where she lives with her husband, Robert, and daughter, Muslimah.

IRVING KARCHMAR
THE MOON IS ALWAYS FULL

The moon is always full
Our human eyes
See only its phases

Love is always here
Our human heart
Sees only its shadow

Joy is always present
Our human mind
Reasons it away

God is always near
Our human spirit
Knows this without words

O Moon, display your full beauty
to my inner eye
O Love, come into the light that casts
no shadow
O Joy, overflow my cup of reason
with your wine
O God, fill me, fill me, fill me
with Your knowing

That my heart may rejoice in You
My eyes may be filled with You
My reason overcome by You
My spirit abound in You

Ameen!

Irving Karchmar has been a writer, editor, and poet for many years, and a darvish of the Nimatullahi Sufi Order since 1992. He is the author of *Master of the Jinn: A Sufi Novel,* and also writes the popular Darvish blog. He currently resides near New York City.

http://www.masterofthejinn.com and http://darvish.wordpress.com

JAMILAH KOLOCOTRONIS
BECAUSE SHE BELIEVES...

The covered woman bows
Down to the God Muhammad worshiped
Touching her forehead to the ground
Touching her heart to the Unknown

The covered woman learns
About life as Muhammad taught it
Opening her mind to obedience
Opening her spirit to love

The covered woman leads
Others to the way Muhammad followed
Doing right and shunning the wrong
Submitting to the Creator

The covered woman lives
In the manner of Prophet Muhammad
Following his perfect example
Being a Muslim

Jamilah Kolocotronis is the author of seven books, including the non-fiction work, *Islamic Jihad*, her first novel, *Innocent People*, and the five-book Echoes Series. *Silence*, the final installment in the Echoes Series, has been recently published.

In 1985 Jamilah earned her Ph.D. in Social Science Education. For twelve years she taught social studies to middle school and high school students at an Islamic school. She and her husband have raised six sons, and they also have two granddaughters. Jamilah lives with her family in Lexington, Kentucky.

S. E. Jihad Levine

The Last Sermon – Ninth Day of Dhul-Hijjah, 10 A.H. Far From the Family Fold

The Last Sermon
Ninth Day of Dhul-Hijjah, 10 A.H.
by S. E. Jihad Levine

Just as Martin Luther King, Jr., told his followers
That he might not go with them to the Promised Land,
Our Prophet Muhammad (peace be upon him) told the Muslims
That after that year he might not be among them again.

He started with "O People, lend an attentive ear,"
Wanting to ensure that they could hear
Words to be taken to those not present that day,
Advice to keep the Shaytan at bay.

He told us that no race is better than another
And that each and every Muslim is our brother.
He said to hurt no one, so no one would hurt you,
And reminded us of the rights of the women too.

He warned of taking usury, and being regular with Salah
For on the Last Day, we will all meet Allah.
He encouraged us to make Hajj, and pay the charity
To dispel the pain, inequity, and disparity.

He asked us to pass on his words to others,
As for more prophets, there would not be another,
After he was gone we were not to stray
The Qu'ran and his Sunnah we are to obey

Oh Rasulullah!
Nabi, Perfect Messenger!
Mercy to Mankind!

FAR FROM THE FAMILY FOLD BY S. E. JIHAD LEVINE

I forgave you for not telling me
when my father died,
I never let you know
how many tears I cried

By my own blood family
I was cruelly betrayed,
Even my husband and friends
were thoroughly dismayed

You claimed you were respecting
the wishes of his wife,
By not letting me know he
was at the end of his life

You admitted you were wrong
and said you were confused,
But the right to attend his funeral
I was refused

Now your daughter, my cousin
has gotten engaged,
My desire to come to the
wedding has you enraged

The thought of your Muslim niece
coming to the Jewish service,
Dressed in garb, wearing hijab
has gotten you nervous

How would you explain it
to all of your friends?
If it offended them
how could you make amends?

Concerned with appearances
and how it might look,
You removed my picture
from the family scrapbook

My conversion to Islam
you cannot accept,
Far from the family fold
I have been kept

L'chaim to my cousin
on her wedding day,
To keep the family peace
I will stay away

S. E. Jihad Levine, Sister Safiyyah, is the 2009 – 2010 Director of the Islamic Writers Alliance. She is primarily a freelance journalist, and has had journal articles and poems published in both online and print venues. As well, Sister Safiyyah is a professional editor. She lives in Pennsylvania with her husband and three cats, and serves as Muslim Chaplain for the Pennsylvania Department of Corrections, SCI Muncy.

She blogs at http://www.shaalom2salaam.blogspot.com. Sister Safiyyah plans to publish her first book in early 2010, Insha Allah.

J. Samia Mair

Iron
"Milk"

Iron by J. Samia Mair

Raw from the mountain, refusing to bend
Brilliant red on the horizon
Your strength is deceiving
A moment exposed you burn and rust
Like blood
A reminder all was created to die
Yet you wax proud as if there is no end

Or do you desire fire to make you pure
Red hot and molten
Flowing without resistance
Completely at the mercy of the Artist's hand
Like a stream traveling down a mountain
Humble, knowing its course
Your destiny will soon be clear

Why scatter aimlessly, burdening the earth from which you rose?
Why suffer in eternal regret, pleading for another chance to die?
Why cease to exist when life dwells within you?

Like a stone hitting iron releasing sparks
Your heart waits to be ignited
But a spark left unattended blackens to ash
And a heart unpolished will surely rust

Streaks of white race across mountains
Beauty and desire side by side
Silver, soft and yielding in the Artist's hand
Smooth, reflecting light
The moon reveals the majesty of the sun

To the few seekers in the dark
But most praise only the color

Beauty waits beneath the rust
Unveil the mystery in your heart
Prostrate like streams returning home
And fear not the stones in the river bed
They are stones releasing sparks

"MILK" BY J. SAMIA MAIR

Inspired by:

Allah's Apostle said, "While I was sleeping, I saw myself drinking (milk), and I was so contented that I saw the milk flowing through my nails. Then I gave (the milk) to 'Umar." They (i.e. the companions of the Prophet) asked, "What do you interpret it?" He said, "Knowledge." (*Sahih Bukhari*, Volume 5, Book 57, Number 30)

Milk
White, Pure
Flowing, Nourishing, Sustaining
A Sign of You
Knowledge

J. Samia Mair is a freelance writer, who has published fiction, nonfiction, and poetry in magazines, books, and scientific journals. Her writing covers a variety of topics, including Islam, public health, and law. She regularly contributes to *SISTERS* and *Hiba* magazines and has her own column, "Tea Talk," in *SISTERS*. Mair is also the Baltimore Muslim Examiner for the online magazine *examiner.com*. Two children's picture books, *Amira's Totally Chocolate World* and *The Perfect Gift*, are expected to be published in 2009. She is a member of the Islamic Writers Alliance, Muslimah Writers Alliance, and National Writers Union.

Uzma Mirza

Blue Fly, *Lullaby*
Orange Blue, *Lullabye*

Blue Fly, Lullaby by Uzma Mirza

In each restless rustling leaf unfolds a subtle harmonic hue,
'He' bestows these specs for you to 'see',
From upon a tree uncloaked, the earth and its' infinity;
She saw the whirling world wandering in you,
Behold, a warm word of a cool morning Spirit Score,
She nurtured you to 'seek', His resplendent Score!

As the universe colors shadows of her children,
Like a snowflake she then ascends,
leaving grains of heavy laden clouds, on your shore,
Sailing over weathering waters she tears no more;
A shimmering silhouette she passes this moment a butterfly,
"As the pale yellow moon illuminates you to not sigh.

Your blueberry palette kneads you to dream,
This memory shore she instilled in you to simply swim,
As her fairy bosom bequeathed a savory sustenance stream,
So sweet she nurtured from within, upon your variegated whim,
building blue tales for your magical spin,
With His song she cradled you to sleep;

Awaken! You reap the world so fresh an eye,
as she beckons your fluttering wings to fly!
In spirit every moment a resplendent flower,
Amidst this meandering memory stage shower;
Dilate your tonal chords of your singing tapestry,
"He" fashioned you in an isochronal majesty to see!

To glorify the colors of His Names,
she breathed into your heart,
From 'His' morning Zephyr Spirit,
A song to enliven your path, not tear apart;

As the nightingale sings this score lit:
"Oh dear child your Mother is near,
And your Father sails whistling the waters without fear."

Upon each shadow stone she slumbers to the sky,
A farewell melody "He" speaks you to not cry,
For the soul of her reverie continues in your 'eye',
'Tis once upon her blue dream,

as 'God' cradles you to 'be'…
For she is in you like a tapestry ream,
flowing…
A lullaby,
…such a prolific, eye.

Orange Blue, Lullabye by Uzma Mirza

Along the edge of this Long shore Sound,
Of a soaring mechanical breeze blue to me;
Came this stroll, with these specs I see;
Spanning wings above, in the blue sky,
Whistling a tune to catch this glancing eye;
A breeze flew by her orange scarf silhouette,
Fluttering a shadow flavor, on the ground,
This mechanical Blue, he gallantly galloped his orange mane around;

As he hovered the blue with no cloud to hide his flow,
he displayed a dance to her motions glow;
In a variegated stance she focused to his every breeze,
Roaming gracefully to his orange bride,
This Mechanical blue wandered in a searching shore stride;

Once upon her dream a flight sang these strings,
A song in green foliage unfolding to grow,
A plight of two souls to each 'He' only knows;
Behold, a bluebird shy, rolling away upon a blue sky,
In my teardrops eye, I sigh.

The sun's golden rays resplendently shine his orange mane,
This scarf reflects his palette stain;
She moves stealthily, to the rocky garden green,
Flying to float with the gull's respite in between;
A blue rain, drops in her path this moment's glitch,
Flying to find her enameled niche;
She regains 'His' eye to ponder herself, inside a falling crystal flake,
To see resounding reverberations rejoicing their "ticking" make,
a rustling a glory of God's Names she proclaims!

As a complimentary tone hailing humbly to the heaven, with her hands,
Breathing her Creators song she stands;
Upon a magnifying spec his flight departs,
Perchance she withdraws like an expanding heart,
In awe of 'His' subtle canvas carved creatively,
A little piece of universe fluttering,

From upon this cool whispering art;
Wings of the derailing sea sedate her innocent soul from debris,
Kneeling on her green carpet, she proclaims 'His' majestic folds I see!
Instilled in her heart irregular rhythms do fly,
To her bluebird untold in time "tocking", she passes it by,
From within the deep blue sea,
"As the pale yellow moon enters",

Prostrating she calls 'His' Names behold the sea,
Each drop reflects 'His' Magnificent mile glory;
As the bluebird sings its song
A little piece of creation story,
Thirsty, she breathes a tear,
To not slumber,
Perchance to sleep.

"Oh my little dear"…
Your father has sailed the water without fear.
So just be here,
You fall and you tear 'He' is always near,
To catch you, oh little heavenly dear,
Remember the reflections I've reminded you to say.
Don't dismay,
in 'His' comfort like a constant gardener
Don't be lured but tame your fame,
and Resound the colors of 'His' symphony Names!

Uzma Mirza is a registered and licensed Architect, LEED certified with the US Green Building Council. Originally hails from Canada, a graduate of Carleton University in Ottawa. She has been practicing for 14 years in the USA, with three internationally distinct firms. She is a member of Green Roofs for Healthy Cities, the AIA, NCARB, and the US Green building Council.

Presently, she is principal and founder of a Sustainable and Green Architecture practice called AYN Architect. She is also president and founder of the non-profit, The Pen and Inkpot Foundation. In addition, she is an Artist and a writer. Her Art is called Pen and Inkpot:

a Spiritual Art. Her Art and Architecture are compliments of each other with the thread of philanthropy and written work the constancy. All her work celebrates, as she phrases: 'the stitching of a Sustainable human'.

She is a Muslim woman business owner, building a social entrepreneurship with the environment, people, and spirituality, in mind. She has spoken at various events and has been interviewed with a Radio podcast in Cairo, Egypt and IU, in Bloomington, Indiana. Presently, she's working on a Library for the Lost Boys of South Sudan and various sustainable designs.

BALQEES MOHAMMED

FAITH COMPARISON
HOPELESS

FAITH COMPARISON BY BALQEES MOHAMMED

Hardly a day goes by
    That I don't think in wonder
Of all the time and energy wasted
    In proliferation of one of life's biggest blunders.

"Just believe," they say
    "Without it you're lost"
—Continuing their false claim
    Of the divinity of the trinity-a distortion from ages past.

With no logic whatsoever
    They have managed to misguide masses for ages
Yet a new tide is arising
    An awakening to the falsity of the writing on their pages.

Laymen, priests, scholars and hard laborers
    Are all coming to realize the truth
That the "Gospel Truth" of the gospels
    Is not so real after all – and backed up with sound proof.

They find now to amazing relief
    The simple logic of the pure truth of Islam
Brought in it's complete entirely over 1400 years ago
To strengthen and guide the community of man.

With the Quran as the pure word of God
    And the Sunnah of the Prophet to boot
We will no longer be lost if we strive in sincerity
    To reach heaven through pleasing the Creator – all in suit.

What lies on the pages of the Quran
     Is not only truth of history in reality
But a challenge to all who seek truth and guidance
     To think without prejudice – such perfect clarity!

Verse after verse you will find the appealing reminder
     That the message is no trivial matter
Nor is it cluttered, foggy or confusing
     Self-explanatory, clear, something for those who think – quite
delights the platter.

My message to you, fellow humans of the world
     Who are still clinging to beliefs of old
Is a challenge to your intellect
     Will you—can you—be bold?

Think clearly about what your religion says about the faith
     Does it command you to merely follow
In blindness to it's origin and accuracy
     Perhaps even leading you down a big hollow?

Or does it grant you the freedom and distinction
     Of reasoning clearly with your mind?
Does it offer you the challenge to reason logically
     With solid proofs – and not require you to follow blind?

If not, then I extend to you genuine invitation
     To find out for yourself the satisfying truth
And to experience a definite realization
     Of the tranquility based on solid proof.

That "There is no God but Allah, and Mohammed is His Messenger"
     Upon that you can surely rely
It is the pure revelation directly from Him up above
     Of that no one can ever logically deny.

HOPELESS by Balqees Mohammed

Hiding under my covers
I cried all night
Didn't you know?

Last night we argued
We had a fight
Didn't you know?

Or did you close
Your door
Hoping we'd get quiet and go?

He hit me
I cried out for help
But no one showed.

I tried to hit back
But he stopped me
We both bent so low

Going physical
After the verbal
Fighting...oh no.

I used to love him
He used to love me
Where did all that go?

What about the good times?
Before the bad ones?
Where? I don't know.

What happened?
Everything's gone rotten
I just continue

But he's got me
Trapped...can't get out
Nowhere to go

No shelters here
No public support
Just pain and sorrow

Need to stay in my husband's home
Be a good wife
No hope for a good tomorrow.

The people talk, you know
About a woman who leaves her home
Assuming the worst possible

They just don't do that here.
And no police calls for domestic problems
Cover your face, woman

Don't let the men in
You're loose if you do
You have no shame

Shame on you.

But isn't the shame on him
Who lays his hand on his wife
Then later turns to sleep with her again?

How can she ever trust him again?
How can she look at him?
How can he look at her?

She has blackened eyes now
Bloody nose and all
Crying incessantly.

Called her mother
Yes, she did
But got turned down again

Told her to be patient
Hold out and stay
It's her place, there everyday

She shouldn't have gone out
Without his permission
She should have remained to stay

It's all her fault
Everyone says
Every time she complains

Who to turn to, then
When it was he who did not hold
His temper, his hand, his heavy parlay?

No one to turn to
No one to save her
From her tormentor

Maybe tomorrow she will die
Or maybe
Today

Balqees Mohammed – An American convert to Islam since 1979, Balqees Mohammed draws from her past experiences as a Christian in the west, while also drawing upon her ongoing experiences as a Muslim living in Saudi Arabia to relay her message to her readers. Whether using the genre of fiction or non-fiction, she addresses the many social challenges she sees in the world about her, in an effort to enlighten people to how Islam addresses such challenges, all in an artistic effort to entertain, while at the same time drive home an important Islamic moral. She is also a regular contributor with inspirational articles that expel an Islamic lesson to a website for one of the local chapters of the Islamic Education Centers, which are spread throughout Saudi Arabia and come under the supervision of the Ministry of Islamic Affairs. You can view a collection of some of her articles previously published on this site at her blog: www.life-islam.blogspot.com; or log onto www.islamunveiled.org to read her articles (posted under the name Om Mohammed) and much more.

Enith Morillo

Towelhead
KHULA

Towelhead by Enith Morillo

The ignorance of the passer by
Observing me, a veiled Muslim woman
Wondering if I'm hot or have completely lost my mind
Envying the respect that for my religion I have.
Living peacefully, I'm not bothered by
How many people stare, frown, and even shout. I
Embrace my way of life with love and fervor
Anxious to be amongst the righteous
Desiring to be in the company of the Most Gracious.

KHULA by Enith Morillo

Suffering by his own hands
What must I do, Oh Allah?
Ask him for the divorce?
the hitting is getting so bad.

Writing, shedding tears,
Desperately looking for good *nasiha*.
To fear You, to pray & fast,
To obey my husband? Not against Islam.

Absence, sentiments of loss,
Thoughts of past, present,
and what is to come.
I toss and turn, in the dark,
covers over my head,
so You won't see me cry.

I feel disoriented, cruel & mean,
I feel at the edge, in my sleep.
And then I awaken, to reality,
I'm still lonely, and in a panic.

For as I step onto unknown territory,
It feels scary, and I feel sorry,
To have to miss my chance in *Jannah*
For not following the right direction.

But what direction am I to take?
How to know what is my test?
To shake your throne, and take the blame?
Or hide my face, and live in shame?

Clouds, darkness, and rain,
It's time to make *du'a* again.
To invoke your name, ask your forgiveness,
To hit the prayer mat this evening.

For when I feel lost,
I know, I am not really lost,
but blind of You.
So reveal to my eyes Your light.

Help me put my trust in you,
and my eyes in the afterlife,
to be strong and free myself
from this abusive man.

Enith Morillo – A revert from Venezuela, Enith is an engineer by profession and a writer by passion. Her writing spans from poetry and short fiction, to career-related articles, to essays about women in science and technology. A lover of reading and the written word, she aspires to become a published poet and author, and to contribute to the spread of Islam by translating Islamic works to Spanish. Enith enjoys photography, nature hikes, and learning.

Sabah Negash

Where Memories Are Laid
In Loving Memory

Where Memories Are Laid by Sabah Negash

I turn over in the bed and glance at the clock. 9:30 AM.
My body aches. How long have I been asleep?
How long has it been since I'd gotten out of bed?
The body dent in the bed said a long time.

My head hurts. My eyes are swollen from crying.
It takes awhile before I'm able to pull myself up.
I look at the clock again, it is now 11 o'clock.
I pull my legs over to the edge of the bed.

My feet drop to the floor like heavy paperweights.
I lift my tear-stained face. All I can see in the dark,
gloomy room is your bright smiling face looking back at me,
A face that once brought life and happiness into my world.

But now it is dark. My light is gone.
Vanished, like the reality of a mirage.
How long has it been since my self-confinement?

My lonely reflection in the mirror cries for its loss.
One hundred days it has been.
One hundred days of grief I laid.
One hundred days of tears I paid.

I pull back the heavy curtains of a past gone by.
Living had once lost its meaning,
but now a new light fills the void.
A new life fills my soul.

Suddenly I hear sounds of old,
like a distant memory.
Not too far but just out of reach,
laughter and song, merry and bright.

I will never forget you for as long as I live,
but time has healed.
I will keep your memory close to my heart
where I'll always be able to find you.

❀In loving memory of my dear mother,
(Naimah) Marva L. Taylor 1949~2007❀

In Loving Memory by Saba Negash

When I was young, you helped me grow.
When I was unsteady, you held me close.
When I was afraid, you protected me.
When I was hungry, you made sure I was fed.
When I was sick, you took care of me.
When I was hurt, you kissed the pain away.
When I was helpless, you picked me up.
When I was lonely, you befriended me.
When I was weak, you shared your strength.
When I was wrong, you showed me patience.
When I was down, you cheered me up.
When I didn't know, you taught me.
When I was lost, you were my guidance.
When I was unsure, you encouraged me.

For all the times I needed you, you were always there.
May Allah the Most Compassionate, bless you and have
mercy on your soul.

My Friend,
    My Heart,
        My Strength,
            My Love,
                MY MOTHER.

Sabah Negash was born and raised in Southern California. She
is from a family of teachers and enjoys traveling and experiencing
new things. Her 15-year teaching career has given her the wonderful
opportunity to live and work abroad. It was through her teaching that
she came to love writing and storytelling to encourage good morals
and character in her students. Her love for teaching and her mother's
constant support, love, and guidance have encouraged her to continue
her education in the field of Early Childhood Education.

Hezreen Abdul Rashid
The Wind

Hovering clouds gather
Kittens scamper in search of their mother
The wind whispers through the trees
Murmuring secrets to the flowers and the leaves
High above, the birds hover in the sky
Like particles of dust drifting by
The whispering turns into a gradual humming
A man makes a dash, his papers go flying
Children squeal with utmost delight
Their swings soar high at an amazing height
The wind then sings at a crescendo
Rocking trees to and fro
Gentle raindrops make ripples on the pond
That sets the palm leaves dancing up and down
As the children leave, saying their good-byes
The trees stop rocking and the howling dies
As Allah commands, the whispers are gone
Thus, the wind has sung its final song.

Hezreen Abdul Rashid is a freelance writer based in Kuala Lumpur. She holds a degree in Accounting from the University of Malaya, and she now writes extensively for Islamic magazines in Malaysia. She is an associate member of Islamic Writers Alliance, and she contributes to Houston's Iqra' newspaper and Tri- State Muslim Media. Her love for the written word has propelled her to blog occasionally at http:// malaysiapedia.blogspot.com/. So do drop her a note and read in the name of Allah!

Ponn Sabra

A Soul Mate by Ponn Sabra
Expressions of the Written Word by Ponn Sabra

A Soul Mate by Ponn Sabra

- Can finish your sentences
- Express your inner thoughts
- Accept your deepest feelings
- Appreciate your far-out dreams
- Hug you with a secure tenderness
- Guide you when you are lost
- Encourage you to reach all your goals
- Love you for all that you are
- Calm you in the middle of your storm
- Excite you during your saddest moments
- Be by your side when you think space is what you need
- Afford you space when you need a moment of peace
- Hold your hand when tension fills it
- Debate with you when stubbornness overcomes you
- Challenge you to be your very best self
- Allow you to grow for inner strength to consume your being
- Forgive you when you are wrong
- Please you when you need comfort
- Laugh with you when anxiety fills the air
- Help you when you need your best friend
- Offer affection with great spontaneity
- Fill your void, as two halves equals one
- Extend a prayer each day of your lives together
- Provide a companionship built on trust, honor, and respect
- Give structure through a common faith
- And make love to you so your legacy carries on through family.

Expressions of the Written Word by Ponn Sabra

Only through the Beauty of the written word may

- History be documented
- Policies be established
- Society be structured
- Cultures be shared
- Recipes bring flavor
- Progress be reported
- Science be analyzed

Only through the Art of the written word may

- Emotions be savored
- Creativity be captured
- Faith be inspired
- The subconscious meet the conscious
- Dreams made into reality
- Love dominate hatred
- Legacies linger

Only through the Power of the written word may

- Knowledge be acquired
- Humanity prosper
- Cures heal
- Nations be unified
- Wars come to truce
- Discoveries advance mankind
- Universal concepts overcome all languages.

Only by writing will you have the opportunity to electrify the written word. Write and your own unique voice will be heard for generations to come.

- Dare to express yourself with the written word.

Ponn Sabra is a devout Muslimah who embraced Islam in 1998. Ponn is a best-selling author of *Empowering Women to Power Network*, writer, columnist, and internet marketer, featured in *Marquis' Who's Who International*, *Who's Who of Women*, and *Who's Who of Emerging Leaders*, (2000 - Present). A home-based entrepreneur for 13 years, Ponn empowers women entrepreneurs to action at http://www.EmpowerWomenNow.com. Ponn was a past Administrator of Connecticut's largest Sunday Islamic school, and a full-time Islamic elementary academy. Nonetheless, Ponn's most enjoyable titles are Wife and Home-school Mama to their three daughters.

Ponn is also the Founder/Owner of AmericanMuslimMom.com – a family-oriented online magazine that encourages Muslim Moms living in the U.S. and American Muslim Moms living abroad to share tips, tools, and resources as they raise Mumins (true believers) based on the Qur'an and Sunnah of Prophet Muhammad (peace & blessings be upon him). The community has a large following of non-Muslims, all of whom benefit from Islamic, motivational, educational, practical, and fun articles, reviews, videos, contests, give-aways, and much more (such as the country's only Summer Islamic Reading Program). Logon to http://AmericanMuslimMoms.com for your free gifts today.

Sabera Salam
The Praised One

Bereft is the heart darkened by disdainful clouds
for whom is hidden the praised one's splendour!
Would that they could grasp the tremendousness of his virtues
And savour the sweetness of his rapturous eloquence!

Fear not – protected is he from what they unduly ascribe
The patient and forbearing, favoured and honoured
Sublime in character; the ever thankful slave
Upon whom the angels invoke their blessings.

He who the Generous One chose to confirm life's purpose,
All humanity will gather seeking his intercession.
Come greet and salute him with sincere abundance
The beloved, the Light, the magnificent exemplar!

Let us strive together in reflecting his exalted radiance
Spirits awakened, satiated with passionate conviction.
Hearts that yearn to bathe in oceans of Divine Mercy
Beat in unison with the rhythm of his Faith and love.

Sabera Salam lives in the United Kingdom with her husband and three daughters. For many years she provided support for IWA members by purchasing and selling member-author books in her bookstore, Safa Books. Her husband's Muslim newspaper also provided advertising support for the IWA organization.

Several years ago, sister Sabera made a difficult business decision to close Safa Books. The good news is that she has created a new online business. She creates handcrafted Awrad book covers and msbahas, tasbihs, sibhas (prayer beads), and sells them online at:

http://www.flickr.com/photos/yearningheart/
and blog site: http://yearningheart.com/page6.htm

CAMILLA SAYF
INSPIRED

Inspired to write
I submit to the greatness
And follow my heart
As it leads me to light.

Inspired to be
I proceed to the gateway
And hear my soul
As it teaches me cry.

Inspired to fly
I will never surrender
And give up myself
As they wish I had done.
Inspired to give
I emerge above surface
And spread up my wings
For I know – love's not gone.

Inspired to live
I will always be there
Where roots I have planted
Stay firm in the ground.

Inspired to speak
I shall let my voice out
And see it reach sky
As I know – I go on.

Camilla Sayf is a haiku poet, freelance writer, and the author of "Lebanese Chronicles." She is a former language teacher who finds her conversion to Islam to be her greatest inspiration. Her work has been published in MuslimHeritage.com, Qalam, MuslimWakeUp, DaralislamLive, and Breakthrough. Some of her writing, including "Lebanese Chronicles" and "Innocent Heart," have been translated & published in other languages.

Zakia Iman Shahbaz
Iman Ghazal*

What good is Iman if you don't see?
How it changes your life for all to see.

A wonderful turn of events begins
You ponder positively to see.

Negativity used to get you down
It becomes released with no frown to see

You look inward then outward and forward
Seek and find the peace you would like to see

It's a feeling within that comes without
From a sacred place we would like to see

When there is no guarantee sign to see

Seek, ask and strive for this sacred gift
From the Great Bestower we hope to see

It's a gift given to the chosen ones
Those that HE deems favorable to see.

Iman prays she is among the chosen
Who will find a home in that place to see.

*The Ghazal is a very old poetic form; older than the sonnet.
It dates back to 7th-century Arabia, perhaps earlier, in contrast
to the sonnet, which goes back to 13th-century Italy. The
ghazal is a series of couplets, five or more. Each couplet is
an independent poem, although a thematic continuity may
develop. There is a formal unity derived from a strict rhyme
and repetition pattern. In the last couplet it is customary for

the poet to mention him or herself by name, by pseudonym, or as "I." In all other couplets this is strictly illegal. The Arab ghazal is more concerned with meter and the long line. By contrast, using couplets and stanzas with a break between them is how the Persians adapted the ghazal.

Zakia Iman Shahbaz, an American, is a retired teacher with a Master's degree in Education and a Major in Art, who taught for many years in public and private schools. A world traveler, she has visited many countries in the Middle East, which has contributed to her knowledge and respect for different cultures. In 2005, she founded the Muslim Women Writers Workshop-International in Sharjah, UAE (www.mwwwi.com). She is realizing her dream of writing and illustrating stories about Muslim children with broad universal appeal to readers of all religions and ethnicities. Specifically, she hopes to contribute literature presenting Islamic beliefs and parenting issues in a positive light that will contribute to cross-cultural understanding. Her book, *A Trophy for Bilal*, has recently been published. All of the illustrations and cover design were done by her. She is looking forward to the publication of her latest book, *A Medal for Nabila*.

Mahasin D. Shamsid-Deen
He Heard
Muslim of our Unique Past
Touch

He Heard by Mahasin D. Shamsid-Deen

It's a rare and beautiful thing to be heard
Understood, heeded, and listened to
A cry received by The Best Authority
A two way communication

Our daily Salaah the magnificent reverberation
Six thousand two hundred and five times
A year
Just before we go into sajdah

Ordained with energy and affirmation
In the Holy Quran
That of surety this will and has happened
And also has been responded to

Samia Allah hu le man hamidan
Allah has heard all those who praise Him
Allah has heard
us

Muslim of our Unique Past
From the Play "Stepping in the Right Direction" ©2007
By Mahasin D. Shamsid-Deen

Don't think that because our feet are in a chain
that we're not believers and a muslim just the same
or that we're broken when our flesh you do sear
cause even with bent back, its still only Allah that we fear

don't think cause our feet didn't walk across the sea
that somehow my Islam was left behind me
that in this new land we somehow let everything go
as if the true Religion of Islam, we did not know

once our feet hit the shores the first steps we did take
was to call on Allah and a du'a we make
then we were yanked and yoked and terrorized
our families torn apart, separated and brutalized

For 400 years our Iman and spirit they tried to break
but this was an injustice that we could not take
through mis-education, injustice mean and bold
we still secretly resisted with song and stories told

like the imprint left from feet walking in the mud we did make
clues for our progeny that even enslaved we did prostrate
digging holes to rest our head in sadjah was just one of those ways
or carving our own tombs etched with our forefinger raised

400 years of slavery in America was a middle passage you see
but it was never meant to be the sole thing that defines you and me
our steps may be heavy, feet dragging the road to this deen
but we'll endure whatever test there is to the musta keen

this thing my people went through was just a test for a time
to strengthen our hearts and serve as sign
for other nations and tribes to learn from the lesson
the right steps back to Allah from under the worst oppression!

Touch by Mahasin D. Shamsid-Deen

the warm *tickle* of air on the ear
as your father chants your first adhan
snuggling carefree and joyous
in your mother's ever present arms
hair *smoothed* from your eyes
when crying tears of joy, pain or confusion
the *pressure* of blood rushing fiercely
as your forehead touches the ground in sajdah
fingers *fumbling* and *grazing* each other
as you all reach for dates to break the fast
a *kiss* gently brushing your cheek
as you salaam your sister or brother
the *colliding* of feet and shoulders
as you line up in the juma ah
the *squeeze* of a million bodies
as you all yell out labbak!
the *kneading* and *massage* of your body
as others prepare your shroud
the *crushing* burden of the earth
as you wait to be *raised up*

Mahasin D. Shamsid-Deen is a second generation American Muslimah with degrees in international marketing and public programs. She has been married since 1986 and has three children. Active in the Muslim community, she runs an Islamic school, organizes programs for local masajid, and often serves as a public speaker, conducting educational workshops for organizations.

A writer since childhood, Mahasin has collected data, and then written technical journals for business and schools, handbooks, educational papers, business reports, proposals, grants, and even ghost-writing. In addition, she has written and/or contributed writing to pamphlets and brochures on Islam, Muslim women, public policy, economics, voting rights, domestic violence, and Mohammed Schools.

As a Poet and published playwright, her first play, "One God," was translated into three languages and presented in special audience before the King of Saudi Arabia. Currently, with her own theatre company, her plays are much sought after commodities for Islamic programs and fundraisers. Mahasin's goals are to Impact! Expand! Inspire! Writing the unique history and culture of American Muslims, so it may be preserved as a legacy for all to enjoy and learn!

UMM JUWAYRIYAH
THE RAIN AND ME

I sit and I wonder through thunder
While
Rain drops
Fall
One
By
One
Hitting the earth,
Mathematically
Accounted for –
Significant
To me
For you see –
Each drop
Was placed by Allah's
Decree
How beautiful it would be
To me
To have –
My each and every move –
Ment
Flow rhythmically
Starting with
Bismillah
To Allahoo Akbar over
Through Subhanallah up
By Mashallah down
To Alhamdulee'lah
Submitting and
Manifesting and just
Oozing out
Through
My pores
Nothing more

Nothing less
But this blessed
Deen
I mean
Just
So fresh
And oh so
Clean – truly living
Islamically
I know when some people look
To me
They have
Their negative ones, twos, and threes
I'd be lying
If I said it didn't
Faze me
Or that I wouldn't be
Happy
If they rather had
Praise for me – (astaghfirullah)
Ya Rabee
Remove this vainness
From me
I don't want to meet You
Covered in shame –
With my deeds empty –
Less than plenty
For having done them for
Other than your
Greatness
So with this wudu
I purify my intentions
And call upon You
By the Best of names
Pray janaza over my own
Naf's games
Ending with a supplication

To remain
Steadfast
And
For Allah
To keep me reminded
Of Him as
My First
And
My Last.
That's the contrast
Between the rain
And me
For you see
Now through thunder
I have found clarity

Umm Juwayriyah, also known as Veiled Writer, is an American born and raised Muslim in her late twenties. She has an A.S. in Communications and is currently completing her BA in English at BayPath College in Massachusetts. Umm Juwayriyah has been writing and performing Islamic inspired poetry and fiction for a number of years. She is the former assistant director and website creator for the Islamic Writers Alliance and currently the editor for the New England Muslim Sisters' Association. Umm Juwayriyah's first Urban Islamic fiction book, *The Size of a Mustard Seed*, was published in July 2009.

The lovely illustrations in *Many Poetic Voices, One Faith* are the creative work of the talented artist and illustrator, Shirley Gavin Anjum.

Shirley Gavin Anjum is the illustrator of several MWP book covers and book interior art including The Islamic Rose Books Series, *Grandma & Hijab-Ez Family Activity Book*, *Star Writers*, *The Beautiful Names*, *Ripples*, and *The Gift*, as well as Teacher Study Guides for a number of MWP titles. She is a mother of five and lives in Ireland. She converted to Islam thirteen years ago and finds working as an artist in the field of Islamic Fiction very satisfying and fulfilling. You can see some of Shirley's work at her website: www.zatoon.com

The beautiful front cover design for *Many Poetic Voices, One Faith* was created by the talented IWA member, Nazaahah Amin.

Nazaahah Amin is an aspiring artist/writer/designer. Her most important roles are being a dutiful servant to the Almighty, and a devoted mother. Art, like writing, has always been her lifelong passion.

In 1997, Nazaahah published her first book, *Let's Practice Our Deen: A Handbook for Young Muslim Women*. She published her next book, a children's book, *Jannah's Story*, in 2007. In 2008 she authored and self-published her second children's book, *Khalidah's Khimar*.

Nazaahah received a degree in Graphic Design from Morgan State University in 2003. She started a graphic design company, Ama Designs, in 2007. Nazaahah is very active in many activities and events in her local community. She currently teaches at the Islamic Community School in Baltimore, Maryland. She resides in Baltimore with her young son.

In Loving Remembrance…Sister Naimah

~Naimah~ Marva L. Taylor was born September 10, 1949 to a Christian family and converted to Islam at the tender age of nineteen. She was a writer, singer, educator, and psychologist. She had a passion for theater and traveling. She wrote many plays, stories, and songs throughout her life. "Water, Wind, Earth and Fire" was one of her most well-liked songs. She received her Masters Degree in Psychology and worked as a social worker, educator, principal, and curriculum writer for many years, both in the United States and abroad. She loved children and was a strong advocate of helping disadvantaged and abused women and children around the world. In 1999, she started a school for children from low-income families in Khartoum, Sudan, where they learned to read and write. In 2007, while working in Malaysia, she was diagnosed with cancer. She returned home to be with her family for her final days. She passed away in her home on October 12, 2007, surrounded by her children.

❀Sister Naimah is the mother of IWA member Sister Saba Negash.

Water, Wind, Earth and Fire
by Naimah: Marva L. Taylor

Water, wind, Earth and fire,
Were created in forms as Allah desired.
Created by Him for us,
Created by Him for us.

In a house that Auntie bought,
Where I was born and first stood,
Among the many, many lessons she taught,
I learned that I would;
Understand the elements of Allah,
Use them for all seasons.
Respect all these elements of His
And waste none for any reason.

Water, wind, Earth and fire,
Were created in forms as Allah desired.
Created by Him for us,
Created by Him for us.

Auntie used to pray for rain and
Look for wind to turn her mill.
She'd dig the earth without shame, and
Use the fire to light her grill.

She said, "Earth needs water to bear good fruit,
Cause without it Earth's crops would soon die.
Fire needs wind to circulate its heat and
Without fire there would be no light!"

Water, wind, Earth and fire,
Were created in forms as Allah desired.
Created by Him for us,
Created by Him for us.

Auntie said "Ungrateful men
Corrupt elements Allah has made,
Their sinful, wicked, greedy ideas,
Will bring them torture to their graves."

"The contaminated water will become their
drink,
Polluted air for their cool breeze.
The radiation in the Earth will make them
think
Atomic fire has gone off under their feet!"

Water, wind, Earth and fire,
Were created in forms as Allah desired.
Created by Him for us,
Created by Him for us.

Written in 1983 by ~ Naimah ~ Marva L. Taylor

2005-2009 NON-IWA MEMBER POETRY CONTEST WINNERS

2005

Youth Category Winner: The Boy Warrior by Kloude

2006

Adult Category Winner: More than a Prophet by Juli Herman

Youth Category Winner (9 to 12 years):
Beginning to End by Mohamed Ali of Surrey

Child Category Winner (6-8 years):
I Love Mohammed by Sabahat Fatima

2007

Adult Category Winner: Desert Revisited by Yahia Samir Lababidi

Youth Category Tied For First Place Winner:
My Birthday by Raneen Hijazi (age 8)

Youth Category Tied For First Place:
SNOW by Nabeela Dana (age 10)

2008

Adult Category Winner: My Iman Lies Within Me by Sara Younis

Youth Category Winner: What is Iman? by Ayesha Ni'mat Fulani

2009

Adult Category Winner: Earthquake by Mr. Ertan Karpazli

Youth Category Winner: The Pen and the Sword by Saara Khalid

Islamic Writers Alliance
(IWA)

The Islamic Writers Alliance is USA based, professional organization for Muslims involved in the literary arts – published and aspiring authors, novelists, poets, essayists, publishers, editors, translators, illustrators, journalists, spoken word artists, bloggers, and playwrights. We support one another in our goals as writers, whether it be honing our craft, seeking publication opportunities, or promoting our published works to both the Muslim and non-Muslim world. We are dedicated to writing about, presenting, and supporting positive Islamic fiction and non-fiction reading materials, in all genres, for all ages.

The IWA is an inclusive organization and welcomes Muslim men and women of all races, ethnicities, linguistic backgrounds, abilities, and creeds.

The IWA's Goals

1) To promote Alliance members' works to the public, both Muslim and non-Muslim, and to book distributors and retailers.

2) To support unpublished authors in their efforts to seek publication, and promote their works to Islamic publishers.

3) To promote reading and writing creative Islamic fiction among Muslim children, the future authors of Islamic literature.

4) To make regular donations of quality Islamic books to Islamic schools and libraries.

2009-2010 IWA Board of Directors

Director: S.E. Jihad Levine
Assistant Director: Mahasin Shamsid-Deen
Secretary: Balqees Mohammed
Financial Officer: Linda D. Delgado
Marketing Director: Zabrina bint Abu Bakar

Chief Editor for *Islamic Ink* magazine: Umm Junayd bint Naeem
IWA Web Administrator: Umm Junayd bint Naeem

www.ingramcontent.com/pod-product-compliance
Lightning Source LLC
Chambersburg PA
CBHW032010040426
42448CB00006B/568